DAVID R. M

ARTS AND CRAFTS
OF TORRES STRAIT

SHIRE ETHNOGRAPHY

Cover photograph
Turtleshell mask with wig of human hair, seedpot rattles, and
cassowary-feather decoration. Acquired by the Australian Museum, Sydney,
in 1901. Probably from the eastern islands and used in death ceremonies.
(Courtesy of the Australian Museum, Sydney.)

British Library Cataloguing in Publication Data:
Moore, David R.
Arts and Crafts of Torres Strait. — (Shire Ethnography; 10).
1. Queensland. Torres Strait Islands. Handicrafts.
I. Title.
745'. 099438.
ISBN 0-7478-0007-3.

Published by
SHIRE PUBLICATIONS LTD
Cromwell House, Church Street, Princes Risborough,
Aylesbury, Bucks HP17 9AJ, UK.

Series Editor: Bryan Cranstone

ISBN 0 7478 0007 3

First published 1989

Printed in Great Britain by
C. I. Thomas & Sons (Haverfordwest) Ltd,
Press Buildings, Merlins Bridge, Haverfordwest, Dyfed SA61 1XF.

Contents

LIST OF ILLUSTRATIONS 4

1. INTRODUCTION 5

2. THE SEARCH FOR FOOD 14

3. RELIGION AND MAGIC 23

4. RECREATIONS 37

5. PERSONAL ADORNMENT 41

6. TRADE 48

7. WARFARE 50

8. POST-CONTACT DEVELOPMENTS 54

9. MUSEUMS 60

10. FURTHER READING 61

INDEX 62

Acknowledgements

The following institutions kindly gave permission for the use of photographic material: Museum of Mankind (British Museum); Cambridge University Museum of Archaeology and Anthropology; Australian Museum, Sydney; Museum of Victoria, Melbourne; Mitchell Library, State Library of New South Wales, Sydney; the Syndics of the Cambridge University Library; and the Australian Institute of Aboriginal Studies, Canberra.

4

List of illustrations

1. Map of Torres Strait with English names *page 6*
2. Map of Torres Strait with native names and trade routes *page 7*
3. Sketch at Evans Bay *page 9*
4. Sketch of village on Darnley Island *page 10*
5. Canoe at Jervis Island *page 13*
6. Openwork bag *page 14*
7. Palm-leaf basket; mat of banana leaf *page 15*
8. Digging sticks *page 16*
9. Shell hoe *page 16*
10. Coconut water-carriers *page 17*
11. Turtleshell fishhook; wooden harpoon head *page 18*
12. Sketch of canoe *page 19*
13. Conical fish trap *page 21*
14. Pearlshell cutting implement *page 21*
15. Masked dancer *page 24*
16. Turtleshell mask from Mount Ernest Island *page 25*
17. Turtleshell mask, probably from eastern islands *page 27*
18. Wooden mask from northern islands *page 28*
19. Human figure used for tobacco magic *page 28*
20. Double sea-eagle canoe figurehead *page 29*
21. Human face canoe figurehead *page 30*
22. Female figure cut from coral *page 30*
23. Carved stone rain-magic figures *page 31*
24. Wood carving of girl used in love magic *page 32*
25. Wood carving of stingray *page 32*
26. Wood representation of crab *page 33*
27. Wheel-like dance ornament *page 33*
28. Model of ancestor figure *page 34*
29. Stone used in garden magic *page 34*
30. Drum, hourglass type *page 36*
31. Improvised mask of bark *page 36*
32. Bamboo smoking pipe *page 38*
33. Stone spinning top; bamboo dance rattle *page 39*
34. Belt of coconut leaf *page 42*
35. Feather head-dress *page 42*
36. Wood hair comb; wood ear weight *page 43*
37. Nautilus shell head ornament *page 44*
38. Necklace of mixed shells *page 44*
39. Crescentic pearlshell pendant *page 44*
40. Perforated pearlshell breast ornament and head ornament of nautilus shell *page 45*
41. Pair of palm-leaf armlets *page 46*
42. Necklet of shells *page 46*
43. Double fishhook turtleshell pendant *page 47*
44. Men dressed in regalia *page 47*
45. Armguard of plaited bamboo *page 49*
46. Stone-headed club *page 51*
47. Cassowary-feather head-dress *page 52*
48. Drawing of a warrior *page 52*
49. Conus-shell breast ornament *page 53*
50. Modern Malu-Bomai ritual *page 57*

1
Introduction

Torres Strait is an entrancing seascape of volcanic islands, sandy spits, sparkling blue water, submerged reefs of green and brown and pale blue skies. It is also a place of danger with its erratic tides and currents and the tropical alternation of wet and dry seasons, which produces sudden squalls, torrential rains and, very occasionally, devastating cyclones.

The Strait is a shallow shelf (10-15 metres or 33-49 feet deep) between Australia and Papua New Guinea. From another point of view it is a constricted channel connecting two great oceans, the Indian and the Pacific. At the narrowest it is 150 km (93 miles) across and from east to west it extends for about 300 km (186 miles). From this shelf emerge more than a hundred rocky islands and islets, atolls, cays and reefs.

The Torres Strait Islanders are a sturdy, jolly, dark-skinned people who are classed ethnically as Melanesian, though their origins are obscure. When first contacted by Europeans, they seem to have numbered about four thousand and were based on some twenty islands. However, in their nomadic, foraging way of life they frequently travelled in their magnificent double-outrigger sailing canoes (figures 4 and 5), visiting almost all the reefs, atolls and cays in their territories from time to time.

History

From early in the seventeenth century the Islanders occasionally sighted European ships and had sporadic contact and clashes with their crews. After the initial discovery of the Strait by the Spaniard Luis Vaez de Torres in 1606, various Dutch expeditions reached its western fringes. Following the raising of the British flag on Possession Island by Captain James Cook in 1770, a number of British mariners sailed through the Strait, including Bligh in 1789 and 1792, Edwards in 1791, Flinders in 1802 and Lewis in 1836. However, it was not until the 1840s that the people had any substantial intercourse with whites (*markai* or ghosts, as they called them) when it became necessary to survey the Strait for the safety of the increasing maritime traffic between the colonies of eastern Australia and the Asiatic ports.

For this reason in 1844-6 HMS *Fly* and HMS *Bramble* under Captain F. P. Blackwood and in 1848-50 HMS *Rattlesnake* and HMS *Bramble* under Captain Owen Stanley spent lengthy

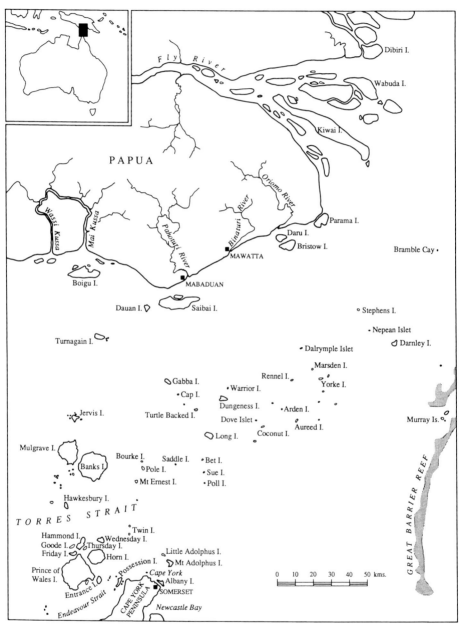

1. Map of Torres Strait with English names.

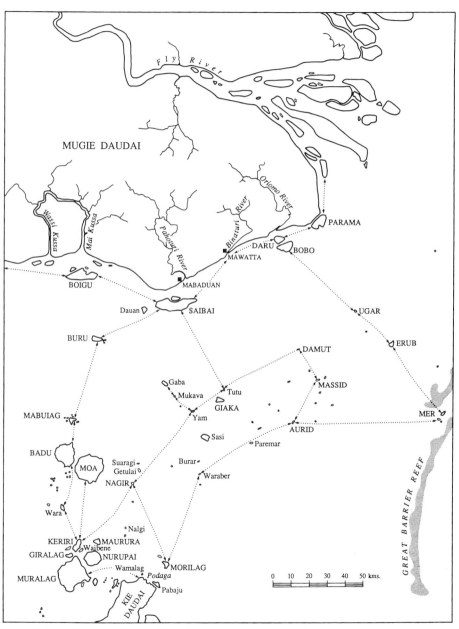

2. Map of Torres Strait with native names and trade routes.

periods at Cape York and among the islands. Relations with both Aborigines and Islanders were close and friendly. The official accounts of these voyages, by J. B. Jukes (1847) and J. MacGillivray (1852) gave the first coherent picture of the Islanders and their way of life. Supplementary accounts (only recently published) by J. Sweatman of the *Bramble* (Allen and Corris, 1977) and O. W. Brierly, artist on the *Rattlesnake* (Moore, 1979) added much valuable detail. An album of sketches by Harden S. Melville of the *Fly* (not dated) shows vividly what the Islanders and their villages looked like prior to European influence (figure 4).

The period following these surveys (1850-70) is poorly documented, but it was undoubtedly a catastrophic one for the Islanders, since many freebooters moved into the Strait to exploit the trepang (a holothurian or sea-slug prized as a delicacy by the Chinese) and the trochus and pearl shell which abounded on the reefs. These entrepreneurs set up semipermanent camps and coerced the Islanders into labouring and diving for them. There were undoubtedly many encounters in which both Islanders and Europeans were slaughtered. There were also frequent wrecks, as the Strait was used by an increasing flow of cargo and passenger vessels, and the Islanders obtained many European goods through trade and salvage.

In 1863 an attempt was made to control this chaotic situation by the establishment of the small settlement of Somerset on the Cape York mainland, opposite Albany Island. Although this became a meeting place for Islanders, Aborigines and Europeans, it did little to regulate activities in Torres Strait itself. This did not happen until 1871, when the London Missionary Society began to found mission stations on the main islands. These, mostly run by Melanesian or Polynesian converts, introduced new cultural traits and vocabulary; some miscegenation also resulted. The Islanders were rapidly converted to Christianity and settled in regular villages around the churches and mission houses.

In 1877 the Queensland Government moved its administrative headquarters from Somerset to Thursday Island in the Prince of Wales group and the traditional way of life soon became only a memory in the minds of the older people. The growth of a major pearling industry, based on Thursday Island, during the last two decades of the nineteenth century turned Torres Strait into a melting pot of races, with the introduction of Malays, Japanese and Pacific islanders as divers.

3. Owen Stanley, Commander of HMS *Rattlesnake*, sketched these western islanders and huts at Evans Bay, Cape York, in October 1849. The man in the centre holds a bamboo smoking pipe and the little boy is bringing him a firestick to light it. The small canoe on the left is a mainland Aboriginal one, much smaller and plainer than those of the Islanders (compare figures 4 and 5). (Mitchell Library, Sydney.)

Anthropological research

The name that stands pre-eminent in anthropological studies in Torres Strait is that of the British anthropologist Alfred Cort Haddon. He first visited the Strait in 1888-9, while Professor of Zoology at the Royal College of Science in Dublin, in order to study the marine biology of the reef systems. While spending considerable periods with only Islanders to help him, he became fascinated by their tales of the old days before the white men came and began to record information and collect artefacts; it was this experience that subsequently decided him to change his speciality to anthropology.

This he managed to do in 1895, by obtaining an appointment as Lecturer in Physical Anthropology at the University of Cambridge, where he had graduated in comparative anatomy in 1879. He then set about organising a multidisciplinary research team to accompany him back to Torres Strait to record all aspects of the traditional life, before the knowledge disappeared. In 1898 he finally assembled sufficient funds and personnel to return to the Strait, where his party worked on various islands for five months. The findings of this expedition, which included psychologists, a

4. This village on Erub (Darnley Island) was sketched by Harden S. Melville, artist on HMS *Fly*, in 1845. Due to their rich soils, the eastern islands carry a much lusher vegetation than the central and western ones. This sketch gives a vivid idea of the life of a pre-contact village and the size and importance of the canoes. (Reproduced from H. S. Melville, *Sketches in Australia . . . During the Years 1842-1846*, London, not dated.)

musical expert and a linguist, and used both moving film and sound-recording equipment, set a new standard in scientific anthropology. The *Reports of the Cambridge Anthropological Expedition to Torres Straits*, published under Haddon's editorship by the Cambridge University Press in six large volumes between 1902 and 1935, have become a classic and the artefacts collected by the team are among the most comprehensive and well documented ever assembled from any ethnic group.

A number of the Haddon artefacts are used to illustrate this book and the account of the way of life of the Islanders that follows draws extensively on Haddon's findings.

The old life

As is the case with most subsistence peoples, so with the Torres Strait Islanders: virtually all of their artefacts were beautifully crafted and adorned with various types of decoration, usually of totemic or magical significance. This makes it difficult, if not impossible, to draw a strict line between art and craft. The problem will be avoided by giving here a brief outline of their traditional lifestyle and then considering in more detail those specific aspects which particularly incorporate both arts and crafts.

Although the Islanders shared a similar marine-oriented way of life and a religion based on totemic hero cults, there were definite variations which accorded with the particular areas of the Strait they inhabited. The westerners, whose high islands are formed of old volcanic rock producing leached infertile soils, were essentially nomadic, moving about almost continually in their canoes as the land and sea foods came into season (figures 3 and 5). The central islanders, whose habitat contains mainly infertile sand spits and cays, were also very mobile and depended greatly on trade to augment their own meagre resources and shortage of drinking water. The northerners, whose low islands lie close to the Papuan coast and are composed principally of silt from the mainland rivers, did cultivate basic root crops quite extensively. They solved the problem of the salinity of their soils by trenching and piling up earth into mounds and ridges. They were the intermediaries in the long-distance trading with the Fly River people from whom came canoe hulls, drums, bows and arrows and items of ceremonial regalia, in exchange for the coveted shell ornaments and adorned human heads supplied by the Islanders.

The eastern people, known as the Meriam, whose islands are composed of more recent volcanics producing rich brown soils, were enthusiastic and efficient gardeners and were much less dependent on the sea for their subsistence. They lived in permanent villages and were altogether less warlike and more sedentary than the other groups (figure 4).

The Islanders all believed that their ancestors had colonised the islands from the Papuan coast. However, there is a curious linguistic anomaly in the Strait, which has not yet been satisfactorily explained. The people of the western, central and northern islands all speak a language which Haddon called Mabuiag (now renamed Kala Lagaw Ya) which is undoubtedly Australian Aboriginal in construction, though there is an overlay of Melanesian phonology. The easterners, on the other hand, speak Meriam Mir, a variant of the current western Papuan dialects. This would seem to imply that the speakers of Kala Lagaw Ya must have had intermixing, or at least extended contact, with Aboriginal people from the Australian mainland at some point in prehistory, whereas the easterners are a more recent arrival from the Papuan mainland. Little archaeological work has been done in the Strait, but so far indications are that the Islanders have been there for at least 2000 years.

The religion of the Islanders emphasised the propitiation of mythical ancestors, who were believed to have travelled through the islands from west to east, endowing the people with the knowledge necessary to survive. They also instituted the cere-monies of initiation and death, in which were featured chants and dances, as well as elaborate costumes including huge composite turtleshell masks and head-dresses. These last are the best known component of Torres Strait art, since they are represented in museum collections all over the world. However, the Islanders also used stone and wood carvings, shaped and incised shells of all types and many other objects, both manufactured and natural, in their rituals and magical procedures.

In their everyday life they employed a great range of tools and implements manufactured from wood, shell, stone and plant fibres. Elaborate incised and painted decorations include series of triangles or diamonds, concentric inverted Us, continuous V incising or fretting, chevrons, conventional star shapes and stylised human and animal outlines. Such decorations appear frequently on canoes, harpoons, bamboo smoking pipes and containers, shell body adornments and innumerable other arte-facts.

The Islanders also made beautiful woven mats and bags and incorporated woven and plaited plant fibres in many everyday and ritual items. They utilised virtually every natural product of their environment, both land and sea, and also added many exotic materials acquired by trade from as far afield as the New Guinea Highlands.

There were friendly alliances and trading partnerships, but also long-standing hostile relationships between both groups and individuals, leading to feuding and raids in which heads were taken. These were dried, adorned and highly prized; they were also a valuable article of trade.

The lives of the island peoples followed the annual cycle of the seasons and the daily round of food-gathering was broken periodically by the pleasure and excitement of ceremonies and trading expeditions. Sometimes it was disrupted less pleasantly by unexpected raids. However, in the main the life of the Islanders was a busy and fulfilling one. Entrepreneurs could build up possessions through trade and marriage, men could acquire ritual status in the performance of the periodic major ceremonies or by skill in magic. Both men and women could make artefacts of utility and beauty, and adults and children took part in lively and amusing pastimes.

5. Professor A. C. Haddon photographed this canoe on Mabuiag (Jervis Island) in 1888. While it was lying on the beach, he asked the crew to set up all the rigging and sails and to take up their usual positions when at sea. Note how the sails can be trimmed with various halyards. There are two steersmen with paddles in the stern. (Reproduced from volume 4 of the *Reports of the Cambridge Anthropological Expedition to Torres Straits.*)

2
The search for food

In their traditional way of life the Islanders were finely adjusted to their tropical marine habitat, with its alternating wet and dry seasons. Exploitation of land foods was mainly the task of the womenfolk. For their collecting activities they manufactured a variety of bags and baskets, ranging from the large, pliable openwork bag called *walsie lie* (figure 6) to a small, stiff palm-leaf basket (*kuta*) used for carrying small amounts of fish, shellfish, crustacea, fruits and nuts (figure 7).

The large bag was made by tying longitudinal stems of a marsh reed (*Lomandra banksii*) with fine cord of plant fibre. It was slung from the forehead by a plaited band and used in the dry season for carrying large quantities of yams (*ketai*), which occurred naturally in the rocky heights and were also cultivated in gardens; in the wet it was employed mainly in gathering the sprouts of red mangrove (*Bruguiera gymnorhiza*) which provided basic carbohydrate when yams were unavailable. The pith of the mangrove sprouts and some yams were toxic and the *walsie lie* bags were also suitable for leaching them in a stream or hanging them from a branch in heavy rain for about 24 hours. These bags

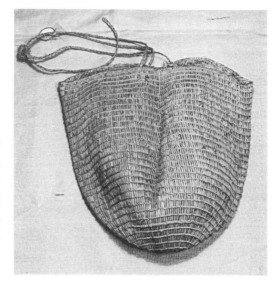

6. This type of large open-work bag was called a *walsie lie*. It was used by the women for collecting yams, mangrove pods, shellfish, and so on. When full, it was carried on the back with the sling around the forehead. It was also useful for leaching toxic foods. Collected in the western islands by A. C. Haddon in 1888. (Museum of Mankind. Photograph by the author.)

7. (Above) Known as a *kuta*, this form of check-weave palm-leaf basket was mainly for carrying yams or fruits. The decorative bands are of red and green cotton strip. The handle is of plaited coconut fibre. Collected on Mabuiag (Jervis Island) in 1888. (Below) Soft mat of twilled banana leaf (*kuri*) used for wrapping small objects and for babies to lie on. Collected in the eastern islands in 1898. (Cambridge University Museum of Archaeology and Anthropology. Photographs by Henry Brewer.)

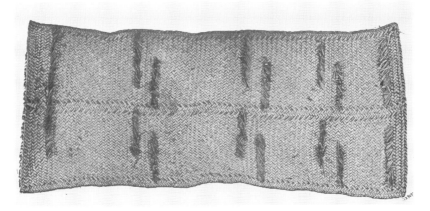

were used, in addition, for gathering oysters and other shellfish around the foreshores.

The women were responsible, too, for making various types of mats. These were vital to the nomadic way of life of the Islanders, particularly those of the western and central regions. The largest mat (*waku* or *moder*) was made by weaving double strips of pandanus leaf in a check pattern. Usually about a metre (39 inches) wide, these mats could be continued indefinitely according to need. They were placed over a framework to make temporary shelters (see figure 3), used for sleeping and sitting on and as blankets; most importantly, they formed the twin sails of the canoes and served as a windbreak or shade on the stages of the canoes. Sometimes they were even employed for catching fish, in lieu of nets, which the Islanders did not make.

Mats were also important for less mundane functions: they formed a secret enclosure for initiates, defined the clan areas for ceremonies and were laid out as a sign of respect to visitors or trading partners.

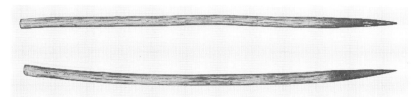

8. A pair of digging sticks (*potar* or *wet*) of light strong wood, fire-hardened at the sharp end. Used by women for digging up roots, tubers, and so on and for preparing ground for planting. Eastern islands, 1898. (Cambridge University Museum of Archaeology and Anthropology. Photograph by Henry Brewer.)

9. Shell hoe for cutting scrub when clearing for gardens. The segment of *Cymbium* shell is wedged in the recess in the wooden handle. Eastern islands, 1889. (Museum of Mankind. Photograph by the author.)

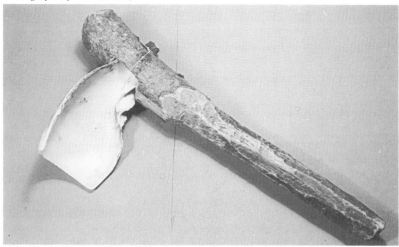

10. Two scraped-out coconuts used as water-carriers. They were suspended from the shoulders by means of the plaited sling, knotted into holes at the 'eyes'. Eastern islands, 1898. (Cambridge University Museum of Archaeology and Anthropology. Photograph by Henry Brewer.)

Small mats of soft palm-leaf (*minalai* or *kuri*) were woven in twilled patterns (figure 7) and were used for wrapping, sitting or sleeping; they also formed cradles for babies.

Two other artefacts were vital in the women's quest for food: their digging sticks (figure 8), shaped on a slight curve from strong wood, with points hardened in the fire, and their small hoes (figure 9). These latter had a blade of ground shell (*Cymbium* or *Tridacna*) set in a wooden handle and were used for cutting scrub and clearing for gardens. Axes and adzes, made in similar fashion, were employed mainly by the men when working on canoe gear or making implements and weapons. For smaller cutting tasks sharpened shells or flakes of quartz were used. In addition, boar tusks, obtained from Papua, with one end ground to a sharp edge, were used for smoothing shafts of harpoons and similar tasks.

Obtaining fresh water (also the responsibility of the women) was a perennial problem. The usual way of transporting it over any distance was in pairs of hollowed-out coconuts supported on a strap of woven palm-leaf and strung from the shoulder (figure 10). For carrying water over a short distance, and for storing it, a large melo or clam shell was used. Such shells also formed the cookpots (*bu*). Lengths of bamboo served a number of functions: carrying, storing and heating liquids, serving as smoking pipes and as flutes and other musical instruments (see chapter 4). Often such bamboos were decorated with complex incised designs

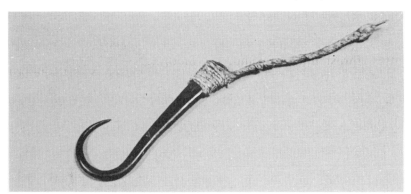

11. (Above) Unbarbed turtleshell fishhooks were in universal use by both men and women, until the iron-barbed European type became available. Bait was tied on. Lines were made by the women in a two-ply twist of coconut fibre. Eastern islands, 1889. (Museum of Mankind. Photograph by the author.) (Below) A harpoon head, cut in hard brown wood with nine barbs. When hurled into dugong or turtle, it detached itself from the shaft and the strong line tied to it allowed the animal to be drawn in. Collected in Torres Strait, probably in 1898. (Cambridge University Museum of Archaeology and Anthropology. Photograph by the author.)

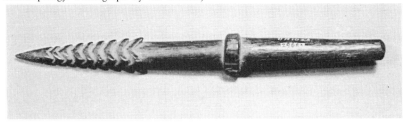

infilled with black.

The women had a further very important task, that of manufacturing the wide range of cords and ropes that were essential to the maritime activities of the Islanders. A two- or three-ply twist of coconut fibre made an extremely strong cord used for innumerable purposes, from fishing lines to stays, lashings and mooring ropes for the canoes. Various types of rain-forest vines were plaited to make the heavier cables necessary for catching turtle and dugong and for anchoring canoes.

The men's part in food production was almost wholly dependent on the canoe, the pre-eminent Torres Strait artefact (figure 5). With a hollowed-out hull up to 15 metres (49 feet) in length, double outriggers, bow and stern posts and wash strakes attached, and with their twin mat sails supported on masts in the prow, these craft were remarkably seaworthy in the hands of mariners as skilled as the leading men in all Torres Strait communities. When not under sail, the canoes were propelled by paddles or poles, the former being used for steering too and the latter, thrust into the sand, for mooring.

The people were continually travelling around the islands and reefs, hunting turtle and dugong, moving camp according to the occurrence of land and sea foods, visiting friends, arranging marriages, making trading trips, going on headhunting raids. Only in the worst stormy periods of the north-west monsoon were they forced to settle in one spot and consequently often went hungry.

Many arts and crafts were involved in the maintenance and decoration of the canoes. For example, the sails and cordage were woven by the women, as already mentioned, while the caulking and general maintenance were carried out by the men. The carved and painted figureheads and woven and plaited ornaments incorporating shells, palm spathes and other adornments were contributed by both men and women. The hulls were decorated with incised designs and were painted up for special

12. O. W. Brierly drew this Prince of Wales Island canoe while it was beached at Cape York in 1849. The sketch shows clearly how the stage and lockers were fixed over the outrigger poles and how the various decorations were devised. The incised design on the prow seems to represent a crocodile. (Mitchell Library, Sydney.)

occasions (figure 12).

Sometimes voyages of up to 100 kilometres (62 miles) were undertaken by the leading men, for trade or to fulfil obligations. The canoes are reported to have attained about 8 knots when running before the wind and took in a good deal of water, which was bailed out with a melo shell or palm spathe. When moving camp each canoe could carry a dozen or more people and considerable quantities of mats, shell cook-pots, poles, spars and ropes stored in lockers of woven bamboo strips on either edge of the central stage (figure 12). Much interesting detail about canoe voyages is given in O. W. Brierly's journals (in Moore, 1979).

The weapons and implements employed by the men in hunting were specialised and beautifully finished. The harpoon (*wap*) used for catching dugong and sometimes turtle was a long pole, up to 4 metres (13 feet) in length, with a bulbous end into which a detachable barbed head of hardwood was fitted (figure 11). The shafts were smoothed, polished and carefully balanced, so that the head almost threw itself into the prey. When struck, a dugong dived and a special strong line attached to the harpoon head was paid out until the animal was exhausted. Meanwhile, the shaft remained floating, to be retrieved later.

A range of hunting and fishing spears were also made by the men for particular species; the bow and arrow was used more for warfare than hunting. Sometimes platforms of bamboo were set up on channels particularly frequented by turtle or dugong and a man was left to harpoon them when they appeared. He would be picked up by canoe later.

Turtle were more commonly caught by diving down on top of them and attaching a strong rope around their fore flippers. An ingenious variant was to leash a sucker fish (*Echeneis remora* or *E. naucrates*) on a fine line through its gills and allow it to swim off and attach itself to a turtle. A man then followed the line down and secured the turtle in the usual way.

A neat device made by the eastern islanders for catching small fish like sardines was a conical trap of split bamboo called a *weris* (figure 13). One man held this near a shoal of fish, while another chased them into the trap with a pair of long bamboo poles. Stone fish traps were built off many of the islands.

Line fishing was practised by both men and women, from canoes and off rocks and headlands. Until European iron barbed hooks became available, the type used universally in the Strait was a 'bent-pin' shape cut from turtleshell, moulded by heat and carefully ground and polished to exactly the right dimensions

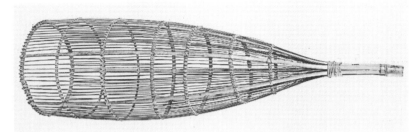

13. A conical trap for catching small fish like sardines. It is made of thin strips of bamboo. One man held the trap near a shoal while another chased the fish in with two long bamboos. These were used only in the eastern islands. Collected in 1898. (Cambridge University Museum of Archaeology and Anthropology. Photograph by Henry Brewer.)

(figure 11). There was a small nick near the top of the shank, into which the line was tightly bound. Bait had to be tied on.

The women did most of the cooking, though the men often helped. Usually it was done in the earth oven (*amai*), a hollow filled with hot stones, on which yams, mangrove shoots, cut-up turtle and dugong were placed, wrapped in leaves. More hot stones were added on top, and sand was heaped over all. Cooking by this method took up to two hours. Neat bamboo tongs were used to lift hot stones and pieces of food. When on the move, or if time was short, foods were stewed in a melo-shell cook-pot over an ordinary fire, but the earth oven was much preferred. Various types of shells were used for cutting up and serving food (figure 14) and a palm-leaf served as a plate.

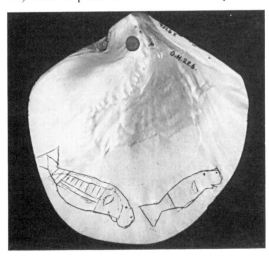

14. Pearlshell with a sharpened edge, probably used for cutting up dugong. The incised decoration shows how this sea-mammal was divided up. Collected on Mabuiag (Jervis Island) in 1898. (Cambridge University Museum of Archaeology and Anthropology. Photograph by Henry Brewer.)

Normally fires were kept alight continuously in camp or village and small fires were carried on pads of clay or damp paperbark on the canoe stages. However, if all fires were inadvertently doused, fire was made by spinning a hard pointed stick between the hands, the point being pressed down into a slab of dry softwood until a smoking dust was produced. By applying dry grass or tinder to this and blowing, a flame could be kindled. In camp, torches of dry bark were used for transporting fire and for illumination at night.

As previously mentioned, the eastern and northern islanders were enthusiastic gardeners, but the western groups seem only to have made gardens intermittently, to augment the supply of naturally occurring landfoods. The method employed in opening up gardens was to burn down the scrub and then pull out the smaller roots with the aid of hoe and digging stick. The whole area was then dug over and the ash mixed into the soil. Yams, taro and other foods were planted and watered, with sticks set up for their support.

Finally, mention must be made of foods obtained by trade. This was especially important for the central islanders, since their islands were unsuitable for any gardening. To compensate for this, they had contacts in all directions and in exchange for what they could produce, such as shell artefacts and seafood, obtained such staples as yams, taro, sago, bananas and coconuts. This was a local form of trading, in contradistinction to the long-distance exchange system for obtaining large artefacts such as canoes, drums and bows and arrows, which is discussed in chapter 6.

3
Religion and magic

Torres Strait religion was based on a belief in mythical ancestors, who were thought to have travelled through the islands teaching the people how to hunt and how to grow various foods; they also instituted ceremonies through which their help could be obtained for the future. Each of the four areas (eastern, western, northern and central) had its paramount myths and culture heroes, but all were linked together in the ancestral journeyings. Also, the totemic clans, with which the heroes were associated, existed throughout the Strait, together with a common system of kinship. This meant that, wherever a person travelled, he could always obtain support from his own totemic group and could identify his own social status, even with complete strangers.

Myths

The predominant myth of the western islanders was that of Kwoiam, always specifically stated to have been an Australian Aboriginal man from mainland Cape York Peninsula who fought with spear and spear-thrower rather than the Islanders' bow and arrow. Kwoiam settled on Mabuiag (Jervis Island) with his family, but later went berserk and raged through the islands and even as far as the Papuan coast, slaughtering and taking heads. He was ultimately cornered on Pulu, a small island off Mabuiag, by a mixed party of warriors from Badu (Mulgrave Island) and Moa (Banks Island), his spear-thrower broke, and he was killed. The cairn where he was buried can still be seen.

The central islanders' core myth was that of the Four Brothers (Sigai, Kulka, Malu and Sau), who arrived from the west and performed various acts of creation for the people. However, during a quarrel Malu speared Sau and as a result the Brothers split up, Malu going to Mer (Murray Island), Sau to Massid (Yorke Island), Kulka to Aurid, and Sigai to Yam (Turtle Backed Island). The people of all the islands knew the complete saga, but their rituals were concerned with the particular Brother who settled on their island.

In the eastern islands the cult of Malu (who also had a secret name: Bomai) encompassed an elaborate and complex series of secret rituals, performed at different places in sequence and culminating in the revelation of the secret masks (figure 50), to the beat of the sacred drum, Wasikor.

15. A. C. Haddon photographed this masked dancer on Thursday Island in 1888. He was taking part in a ceremony to welcome the arrival of the monsoon. The head-dress includes both native and European materials. (Reproduced from volume 4 of the *Reports of the Cambridge Anthropological Expedition to Torres Straits*.)

16. Turtleshell mask, incorporating a crocodile head and a human face, collected on Nagir (Mount Ernest Island) in the central islands, by A. C. Haddon in 1888. It was probably used in death ceremonies. (Cambridge University Museum of Archaeology and Anthropology. Photograph by Henry Brewer.)

The two key artefacts used in the ancestor rituals were masks (or head-dresses) and drums. The latter will be discussed in the next chapter, since they were used just as much in secular dances as in sacred ceremonies, but the possible significance of those secret masks that have survived must be considered here. The western, central and eastern masks are complex constructions of turtleshell plates lashed together and adorned with cassowary feathers, nut rattles and incised decorations. Often intricate fretwork of turtleshell is added around the fringes. Sometimes they portray just a human face (see cover and figure 17), but more commonly they are a composite of animal and human (figures 15 and 16). This was because they were emblems of the culture heroes and their associated totems. The northern masks are generally made of wood, probably because turtle are less common in the muddy Papuan waters, and represent an elongated human face (figure 18). All these masks were used chiefly in initiation ceremonies and funerary rituals.

Initiation

Re-enactment of the cult myths was at the core of initiation, which took place at puberty. The details varied from area to area, but the underlying rationale was universal. The youths were segregated in a secret area (*kwod*) for several months, during which they were instructed in good behaviour, were subjected to trials and ordeals, and were taught the myths appropriate to their group. The climax was a dance ceremony, performed at night by the light of flickering fires, in which initiated men, wearing the huge turtleshell masks and covered from head to foot with grass costumes, performed to the accompaniment of slow chants and the beating of drums. These masks, which may appear grotesque or even comic when enclosed in glass cases in museums, must be judged for their qualities when used in this context (figures 15 and 17). They were deliberately intended to terrify the boys and to inscribe indelibly in their minds all that had been inculcated into them during their months of seclusion and privation. The great amount of work that must have gone into the construction and decoration of these masks demonstrates how important they were to the people.

Once these rituals were completed, the boys were dressed in finery and taken back to their families, where they were greeted as if returned from the dead, congratulated and feasted. They were then deemed to have become men and were ready for warfare and marriage.

The secret ceremonial grounds were usually fenced round with matting and contained stone arrangements, shells, skulls, stone carvings of the ancestors and other decorations of significance. Women and children were forbidden to go near them, on pain of death.

Mortuary ceremonies

The other major activity in which masks, costumes and drums played a part was the mortuary ceremony. Again there were wide variations in detail, but the basic procedure was common to the whole Strait. When a man died his body was carried well away from the camp or village, while everyone wailed and keened in mourning; it was then exposed on a wooden platform. The spirit of the deceased was believed to hang around his body until the correct ceremonies had been performed to release it to depart to the island of the dead, far away in the direction of the setting sun. In the western and central islands the head was later removed for divination to ascertain the cause of death and was subsequently adorned for presentation in a basket to the widow at the major ceremony about six weeks later. This ceremony, called the *markai* or ghost dance, also included masked and costumed

17. The exact provenance of this remarkable mask is unknown, but it was collected in Torres Strait before 1890. It almost certainly came from the eastern islands and may have been used in the death dances (*keber*). (Museum of Victoria, Melbourne.)

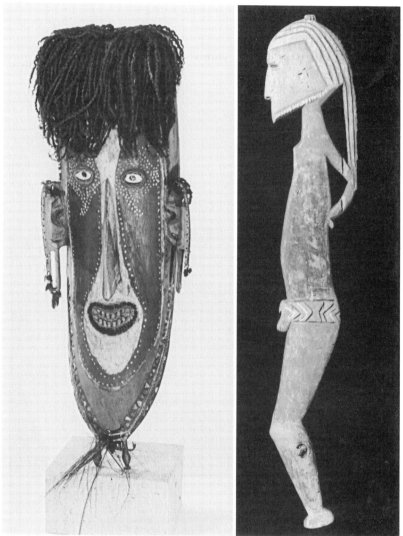

18. (Left) This wooden mask is typical of the northern islands style. It was purchased from the captain of a trading ship in 1885. (Australian Museum, Sydney. Photograph by Charles Turner.)

19. (Right) Silhouette of painted wood placed in tobacco gardens to protect them from thieves and pests. It is coloured red, black, yellow and white. Collected on Murray Island in 1889. (Museum of Mankind. Photograph by Henry Brewer.)

dancers, together with chants and drumming.

In the eastern islands the corpse was tied to a rack and slowly smoked over a fire until thoroughly desiccated. The mummy was then taken out to sea on a canoe and eviscerated and cleaned. Later it was adorned with decorations and armlets, as if still alive, and a whole series of dances (called *keber*) were performed by various relatives. Again masks and long grass costumes were employed. Ultimately the dried hands, feet and tongue of the deceased, together with his belts, straps, pendants and other body decorations were given to the widow, who had to wear them for a year as a memorial. The mummified body was kept in a special hut near the living area and not buried until all the rituals were completed and the spirit finally released. Funerals for women and children were much less elaborate on all the islands.

Magic

Magic (*maid*) permeated every activity of the Islanders, from birth until death, and even thereafter. The leading men were all skilled medicine men (*maidelaig*) and a wide range of artefacts was associated with the various forms of magic.

For example, miniature human figures were set up in gardens, with appropriate chanted spells, to protect them from theft and to promote growth (figure 19). Figureheads, both animal and human, were attached to canoe prows to bring good luck in the chase (figures 20 and 21). Stone figures of pregnant women were placed by fires in a camp or village when everyone was leaving (figure 22). The symbolism is not obvious in this last case: pregnant women and babies were usually left in camp when people went off hunting and collecting, but if there were none available, then the effigies were positioned to deputise in the important duty of keeping the fires alight.

Medicine men believed they could control both wind and rain (an important matter for both gardening and canoe voyaging). In

20. Double sea-eagle figurehead, attached to prow of canoe to gain good luck in the chase. Painted in red, black and white ochres. Collected on Mabuiag (Jervis Island) in 1898. (Cambridge University Museum of Archaeology and Anthropology. Photograph by the author.)

21. (Above) Northern islands canoe figurehead, known as a *dogai*, was tied to the prow of canoe to look out for turtle and dugong. Collected on Saibai in 1898. (Cambridge University Museum of Archaeology and Anthropology. Photograph by Henry Brewer.)

22. (Left) This remarkable representation of a pregnant woman was cut from coral and used magically to keep fires burning when everyone was away from camp or village. Collected on Mer (Murray Island) in 1889. (Museum of Mankind. Photograph by the author.)

the eastern islands an oblong natural volcanic stone, sometimes slightly modified to resemble a man, was a key artefact in rainmaking (figure 23), which also included the burning of banana leaves and the chanting of spells. The bull roarer (a flat piece of wood on the end of a string) was swung to induce a change of wind or to bring calm at times of high winds.

Turning to the use of magic directly to affect human beings, what may be termed revenge magic was practised against enemies, whether within one's own group or in another. A method frequently used was to create an effigy of the hated man or woman, in wood, stone or gum, and then spear it or rub noxious substances upon it, while intoning spells. Sometimes the

23. (Left) A *doiom* or rain-magic figure from the eastern islands. These magic stones are usually modified slightly to resemble human beings. Collected in 1898. (Right) This carved stone figure is also a *doiom* and is unusual in the amount of detail portrayed. It is just possible that it was traded in from the New Guinea mainland, since it has affinities with some of the prehistoric stone carvings found in the New Guinea Highlands. The rounded base suggests that it could originally have been a pounder. Collected on Mer (Murray Island) in 1898. (Cambridge University Museum of Archaeology and Anthropology. Photographs by Henry Brewer.)

24. (Left) This detailed wood carving shows clearly the body scarification practised throughout Torres Strait. It was used in love magic. By rubbing it with sweet-smelling substances and intoning spells, the love of a particular girl would be obtained. Collected in the eastern islands in 1889, but stated to have originated from Massid (Yorke Island) in the central islands. (Museum of Mankind. Photograph by the author.)

25. (Below) Small carving of a stingray in dark brown wood. It was probably worn as a pendant of the owner's totem or to bring good luck in the chase. Collected on Tutu (Warrior Island) in 1888. (Museum of Mankind. Photograph by the author.)

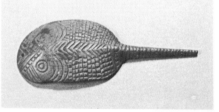

medicine man would creep up upon the victim, whilst asleep, and rub a poisonous substance upon him or her.

Another type of magic in wide use was love magic. In Torres Strait men were not supposed to approach girls they wanted to marry; the girls were expected to start the courting by sending a gift to their beloved via an intermediary. For this reason men frequently carried out love magic to influence the girls of their desire to fall in love with them. The principal method was to make an effigy of the beloved one and then to rub it with special substances, while chanting love songs (figure 24). Another procedure was for the aspiring lover to rub his own body with sweet-smelling oil or bark to arouse a reciprocal emotion in the girl of his choice, when he was dancing before her or passing near her.

Medicine men also had a number of therapeutic techniques, some magical and some practical: for example, people with fever were laid beside a hot fire and water was poured over them to induce perspiration; a particular kind of brown earth was given to pregnant women and young children to eat in order to relieve

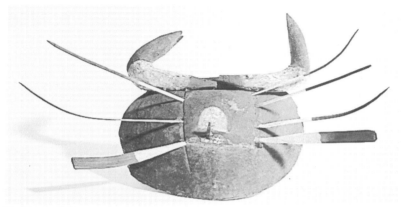

26. This realistic crab, made from light wood and bamboo strips, is painted vividly in red and white. It was carried, perhaps on a stick, in dance ceremonies. Eastern islands, 1898. (Cambridge University Museum of Archaeology and Anthropology. Photograph by Henry Brewer.)

27. Wheel-like dance ornaments, such as this, were used in the central islands. They were held in the hands and twirled in dances. The figure on the central boss is a sucker fish, employed in catching turtle. Tutu (Warrior Island) 1988. (Museum of Mankind. Photograph by Henry Brewer.)

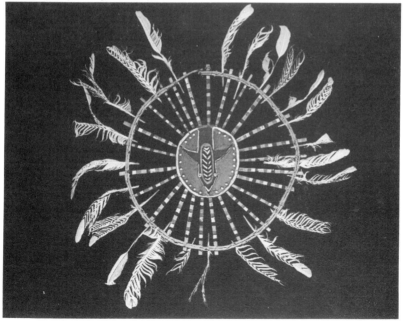

28. (Left) Model of a mythical ancestor called Waiet, made for A. C. Haddon in the eastern islands in 1905. It is a representation of a life-sized turtleshell figure of Waiet which was kept in a cave high in the volcanic cone of the island of Waier, in the Murray group. (Cambridge University Museum of Archaeology and Anthropology. Photograph by Henry Brewer.)

29. (Below) Piece of spongy grey lava remotely resembling a human head. It was painted red and white and used in garden magic in the eastern islands. Collected in 1898. (Cambridge University Museum of Archaeology and Anthropology. Photograph by Henry Brewer.)

indigestion; and blood-letting, by making small incisions with sharp flakes of quartz, was commonly used to relieve aching limbs.

Some further artefacts connected with magical or ceremonial rituals may be described before concluding this chapter. The fact that everyone in Torres Strait belonged to a totemic clan has already been mentioned. Often people carried a replica of their totem, strung from the neck (figure 25) or carried in the hand in the dance (figure 26). In the central islands an unusual type of dance ornament was used in the latter fashion: it was a wheel-like construct of bamboo strips adorned with white feathers, and often had the owner's totem portrayed in the centre or hub of the wheel (figure 27).

It seems likely that in the eastern islands life-sized figures of totemic ancestors were kept hidden. Certainly such a figure of a cult-hero called Waiet was kept in a cave high on the old volcanic cone of Waier in the Murray group and was brought out in annual ceremonies (figure 28). The broken remains of this figure, which was constructed wholly of turtleshell, are kept in the Queensland Museum.

Finally, any natural stone of unusual shape was likely to be linked up with an event in a myth and incorporated into the appropriate ritual. Many such stones were given voluntarily to Professor Haddon at the end of the last century, by which time the old cults had been suppressed by the missionaries. Nevertheless, the Islanders wished their sacred objects to be preserved rather than destroyed by the missions. For this reason a great many have survived for study, though the mythical background to them is often imperfectly recorded (figure 29).

30. (Above) This superb *warup* drum
was purchased from a trader captain in
1886. It has a tympanum of lizard skin
and decorations of cassowary feathers
and goa-nut rattles. (Australian Museum,
Sydney. Photograph by Charles Turner.)

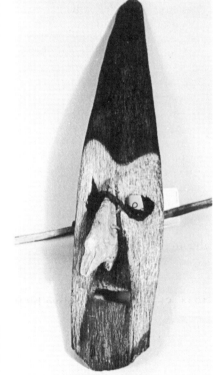

31. Improvised mask of painted bark,
collected by the crew of HMS *Rattlesnake*
at Cape York in 1849. Probably made by
visiting Prince of Wales Islanders for a
recreation dance. (Museum of Mankind.
Photograph by the author.)

4
Recreations

The most popular pastime of the Islanders was dancing. The formalised ceremonial dances described in the previous chapter took place at intervals throughout the year, except during the worst periods of the wet season. There were also improvised secular dances in camps or villages almost every evening, particularly when there were visitors from other groups. These camp-fire dances might commemorate events of the past or things that had happened during the day just ending. The central artefact in all these dances was the drum, which was in almost continual use, and every group had at least one. The traditional drums have proved the most enduring artefacts in Torres Strait and are still universally used in dance celebrations, church services and at funerals. The modern examples are not nearly as elaborate as the traditional ones.

There are two types, the straight-sided, slightly conical *buruburu* type, which usually has a fish or crocodile head represented at its open end, and the *warup*, a heavier instrument cut from solid, dark wood in an hourglass shape (figure 30). These drums usually have a side handle, either cut in the solid wood or attached, for they are sometimes played on the ground but just as often carried by one of the dancers. The tympanum is of dried lizard-skin and is 'tuned' by attaching blobs of hot wax. Probably most of these drums were imported from mainland Papua, since there were no suitable trees on most of the islands, but it is likely that they came in rough form and the final finishing and decorating was done by the Islanders themselves. Often both types were embellished with incised or carved totemic animals and other decorations and attached were cassowary and seabird feathers, goa-nut rattles and other appendages. The drums, like the masks, were works of art of the highest craftsmanship and were greatly valued.

An amusing example of a topical secular dance was reported by Barbara Thompson, a young Scots girl, sole survivor of a wreck in 1844. She was held captive by the Prince of Wales Islanders until rescued by the crew of the *Rattlesnake* in 1849. She described how a visiting party of central islanders performed a 'ghost ship dance' in which they wore masks of natural pale palm-leaf with reddened cheeks and imitated the movements and postures of the whites (Moore, 1979, pages 199, 226). The song they chanted was

translated as:
  Choki (tobacco) eenow good,
  Choki eenow good (said by the sailors as a joke)
  White man ship dance and sing.
  Tobacco biscuit knife,
  They have all gone to get for us.
 A mask collected at Cape York by the crew of the *Rattlesnake* in 1849 (figure 31), now in the Museum of Mankind, is stated to have been used in a 'corroboree' a few nights before and was probably made by visiting western islanders. It could well have been improvised on the spot and used in a 'white man dance'.

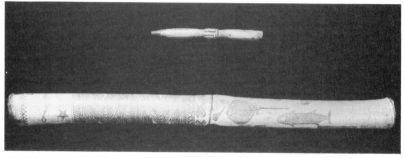

32. (Above and below) Bamboo smoking pipe from the northern islands, collected by C. G. Seligman in 1898. The incised decorations are infilled with charcoal and include a crocodile. The tobacco bowl is carved from soft wood. (Cambridge University Museum of Archaeology and Anthropology. Photograph by the author.)

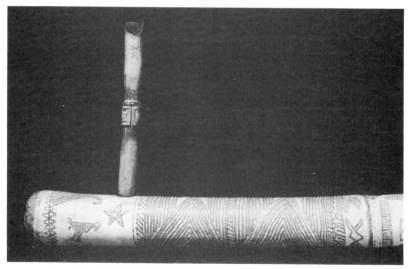

33. (Left) Spinning top with disc of ground volcanic ash and spindle of black palm, used only in the eastern islands for men's competitive game. Painted design of moon and stars. It was kept in the basket for protection when not in use. Collected in 1898. (Cambridge University Museum of Archaeology and Anthropology.

(Below) Bamboo dance rattle. The bundle of rods was pulled with the string through the hole to make a rattling rhythm. Collected in the eastern islands, 1889. (Museum of Mankind.) (Photographs by Henry Brewer.)

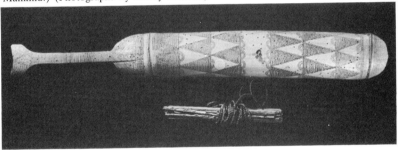

The next most popular recreation was the sociable smoking of tobacco. This was much more of a friendly ritual than it is with most peoples. A light tobacco was grown throughout Torres Strait even before the first historical records and was smoked in a pipe formed of a segment of bamboo between 60 and 80 cm (24 and 31.5 inches) long and about 5 cm (2 inches) in diameter. One end was open and a small tobacco bowl was inserted in a hole in the top. The custom was for one man or woman to light up and draw smoke into the bamboo. It was then passed on to a friend who inhaled the smoke and followed the same procedure for the next person. Apparently the local tobacco was not very strong, but when European 'navy twist' was smoked in this way it caused nausea or even unconsciousness. These bamboo pipes were usually decorated with animals and abstract designs in a fine incised groove infilled with black (figure 32).

Another recreation associated with interesting artefacts was the competitive spinning of large disc-shaped spinning tops, made of finely ground soft lava (figure 33). They were often decorated with painted designs and given names. This game seems to have been confined to the eastern islands, where it was a favourite spare-time pursuit for the leading men. Successful tops were highly prized and kept in special baskets for safety. The stone discs were drilled through the centre and a black-palm spindle inserted. This was spun between the hands with the lower point resting on a piece of polished shell, on which remarkable times could be attained. Smaller tops, made from dried beans of the Queensland matchbox bean (*Entada phaseoloides*) were used by children elsewhere in the Strait. This was probably the origin of the game, since all types of top were called *kolap*, the vernacular name for the matchbox bean.

A popular team game throughout the islands was played with curving sticks or bamboos and a solid hardwood ball. It was known as *kokan* or *kai* and took place on flats and beaches; it seems to have resembled hockey. There was also a handball game, played with a light hollow sphere of interwoven pandanus strips.

Haddon recorded a series of string games, resembling cats-cradle. These were certainly practised by women and young girls in the western islands and were probably universal favourites before European intervention in the Strait. There were songs and stories attached to each string figure.

Apart from the ubiquitous drums, the Islanders used a wide range of other percussion and wind instruments: nut rattles, bamboo and reed flutes, and several types of bamboo rattle, of which the *kerker-keber* was perhaps the most ingenious and well-finished (figure 33). Pierced conch shells (*bu*) were blown for communication and on triumphal occasions.

A number of children's word games, songs and hide-and-seek type competitions were also recorded and children, as every-where, loved models of human beings, animals, weapons, masks and so on.

It is clear from the artefacts and information collected by Professor Haddon and others that the Islanders, in spite of the relentless search for food, had ample time for amusements and recreations and that new songs, dances and games were being invented or adopted all the time.

5
Personal adornment

Both men and women loved dressing up. Normally men went naked, except for perhaps a belt (figure 34), but after puberty women always wore a knee-length skirt of grasses or teased-out bark. However both sexes needed scarcely any excuse for putting on all sorts of adornments of shell, wood, seed, feather and woven plant fibre. Some of these body ornaments were among their most prized possessions.

The men usually wore their hair shoulder-length, but when in mourning it was customary to cut it all off. They then sometimes wore quite lifelike wigs of human hair or ochred grass (see cover illustration). Women had their hair cut short, but some unmarried girls left tufts or ridges of hair to make themselves attractive. Headbands or fillets of woven palm leaf, shells, seeds and so on were occasionally worn (figures 37 and 40). Decorated combs of wood or turtleshell were used for dressing and fixing the hair (figure 36).

For any sort of occasion, such as dances, visits to other groups, trading or warfare, the men put on all kinds of finery. Head-dresses of white seabird feathers or cassowary feathers were worn throughout the Strait (figures 35 and 47). At puberty the ears of both sexes were pierced all around the edges for tying on decorative shells; a particularly large incision was made in the lobe and this was kept open by inserting bi-lobed ear weights (figure 36). The nasal septum was pierced in infancy and the orifice kept open with a small wooden plug. After initiation, youths were allowed to wear nose ornaments of ground clam shell; some were straight, others slightly curved (figure 44).

A variety of necklaces and pendants were worn by both men and women, incorporating pearlshell shapes, unmodified small shells, seeds, turtleshell plates and so on (figures 38, 42 and 43). Only the men wore the half-moon pearlshell breast ornament known as a *mai* or *mari* (figure 39 and see figure 44). These were mainly manufactured in the western islands and were a valuable article of trade with mainland Papua. Another type of breast ornament was used by both sexes; it was known as a *dibi-dibi* and consisted of the ground-down tip of a conus shell, suspended on a band (figures 49 and 44). The Islanders were highly skilled in working pearl and nautilus shell, as can be seen from the pieces illustrated in figure 40. The difficulty in achieving such delicate

34. Belt made of plaited
coconut leaf painted in a
pattern of red and blue. This
is a mourning belt obtained
from the eastern islands, in
1905. (Cambridge University
Museum of Archaeology and
Anthropology. Photograph
by Henry Brewer.)

35. Ceremonial feather
head-dress (*dari* or *dri*) used
throughout Torres Strait. To
a framework of bamboo
bound with string and
painted red and blue are
attached white seabird feathers, cut around the edges to
form a pattern. Some cas-
sowary and other feathers
are also incorporated. Collected in 1898. (Cambridge
University Museum of
Archaeology and Anthropology. Photograph by Henry
Brewer.)

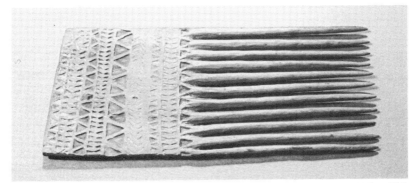

36. (Above) Wood comb with incised decoration infilled in red, white and blue. This type was used throughout the Strait for both combing and fixing hair. Eastern islands, 1889. (Museum of Mankind. Photograph by the author.) (Below) Ear weights were inserted to stretch the incision made in the ear lobes in adolescence. This one is unusual in its incised decoration. Collected on Mer (Murray Island), probably in 1898. (Cambridge University Museum of Archaeology and Anthropology. Photograph by the author.)

work before the advent of steel tools can be imagined. No example of a traditional Torres Strait drill has survived, but they are known to have been similar to the firestick, spun between the hands and tipped with stone or shell. Other pendants were made of turtleshell in a great variety of designs, cut and shaped by heating (figure 43).

Both pendants and armlets were also made from boar tusks obtained from New Guinea, since there appear to have been no pigs in Torres Strait before white settlement there. The most

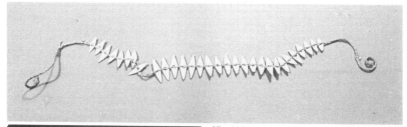

37. (Above) This head ornament of small lozenge-shaped pieces of nautilus shell strung on fine cord was worn by medicine men in the eastern islands. Collected in 1889. (Museum of Mankind. Photograph by the author.)

38. (Left) Elaborate necklace of small mixed shells with a pendant of pearlshell and a red wool tassel. Collected on Murray Island in 1889. (Cambridge University Museum of Archaeology and Anthropology. Photograph by Henry Brewer.)

39. (Below) Such crescents of ground pearlshell with incised decoration were worn on the breast by men for ceremonies and warfare throughout the Strait and were a valuable trade item. This one is suspended on a woven coconut-fibre braid, but often human hairstring was used. Collected on Muralag (Prince of Wales Island) in 1888. (Museum of Mankind. Photograph by the author.)

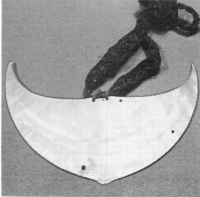

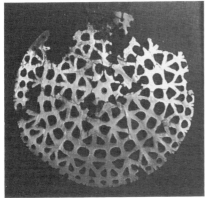 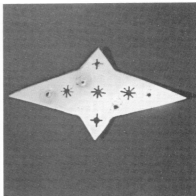

40. (Left) Very rare perforated pearlshell pendant from the eastern islands. Such pendants were worn by the men belonging to the *giri-giri le* (kingfisher men) at the conclusion of the Malu-Bomai secret initiation ceremonies. Collected on Mer (Murray Island) in 1898. (Right) Tiny star-shaped decoration of nautilus shell with fine star perforations and two suspension holes. Worn on the forehead on a headband. This is also from the eastern islands and was collected in 1898. (Cambridge University Museum of Archaeology and Anthropology. Photographs by Henry Brewer.)

valuable artefact for trade exchanges in Torres Strait was a rather uninteresting-looking armlet made of a ground-down spiral cut from a large conus shell. Known as *waiwi* or *wauri*, these were worn by men for ceremonies or warfare. Woven armlets, with shell and other decorations, were worn by men for all special occasions (figure 41) and finger rings and leg bands of plaited coconut root were popular with both sexes.

An unusual necklet was collected by the *Rattlesnake* and presented to the British Museum (figure 42). It was obtained at Erub (Darnley Island), but may have come originally from New Guinea. It is certainly a unique specimen and a product of highly skilled workmanship. Unfortunately it has not been possible to identify the shells from which it is made.

Not only conventional body decorations were used. The Islanders delighted in adorning themselves with any bright flowers, seeds, leaves and shells they happened to find. They also enjoyed painting their bodies with red, yellow and white ochres in elaborate patterns for dances and ceremonies.

Complex body scarification was practised on both men and women. This was usually carried out at puberty, but was not connected with initiation; it was merely an adornment to make the boy or girl attractive to the opposite sex. Haddon recorded an extensive series of the patterns incorporated into these designs,

41. Pair of armlets collected on Mabuiag (Jervis Island) in 1898, but typical of those worn by men on all the islands. They were made of woven palm-leaf; the join is decorated with trade beads and cotton strips. Traditionally, small cowrie shells would have been used with a fringe of the woven leaf. (Cambridge University Museum of Archaeology and Anthropology. Photograph by Henry Brewer.)

42. This remarkable necklet was collected on Erub (Darnley Island) by the crew of the *Rattlesnake* in 1848-9. It is a unique specimen and the craftsmanship involved is of a very high standard. Possibly traded from mainland Papua. (Museum of Mankind. Photograph by the author.)

which varied from shield-shaped incisions on the upper arm to parallel curving lines, bird-like shapes and crossed lines on torso and thighs (figure 24).

Some idea of how the Islanders appeared when dressed up in their finery may be gained by comparing figures 15, 44 and 48.

43. (Left) Double fishhook pendant cut from turtleshell, with incised decoration. Such pendants formed part of the regalia of brides and married women. Collected on Mer (Murray Island) in 1889. (Museum of Mankind. Photograph by the author.)

44. (Below) A. C. Haddon photographed these eastern island men dressed up in all their finery in 1898. They demonstrate the whole range of items worn by men for ceremonies and warfare. (Reproduced from volume 4 of the *Reports of the Cambridge Anthropological Expedition to Torres Straits.*)

6
Trade

The trading system in Torres Strait was not a formalised ceremonial exercise, such as the Kula in the Trobriands or the Motu voyages in southern Papua, nor was it a straightforward bartering system. The most complex aspect of it related to the obtaining of canoe hulls from the Fly River. When a leading man required a canoe, he sent a preliminary payment in shell ornaments, human heads or other valuables to a trading partner in the next group of islands to his north. In the west the route went from the Prince of Wales group to Badu, Mabuiag, Saibai and Mawatta on the Papuan coast, and thence to Daru and the Fly River mouth. The central islands' route was via Yam and Tutu to Saibai, while the easterners had a direct route via Erub, Ugar and Bobo (see figure 2).

The request and part payment would be passed on from one trading partner to another until it reached one of the groups at the mouth of the Fly. Ultimately a canoe hull came back by the same relay system, the double outriggers and wash strakes being added en route, until at last it reached the original purchaser. If he was satisfied, he was expected to send further payments for the following three years.

Obviously such a system depended on total honesty in all participants, but it was understood that each intermediary took a small cut from the trade goods as a recompense for his trouble. When European materials became common in the Strait, canoe payments tended to be made in iron bars, nails, wire, chains and other exotic articles.

Trade with New Guinea was also carried out to obtain drums, bows and arrows and stone clubs, as well as articles desired for ceremonial regalia, such as cassowary and bird-of-paradise feathers and pig tusks. For these goods a single payment would usually suffice, but even then it was never a straight barter, since the transaction involved a whole string of relationships along the way. The far-reaching nature of this exchange system is demonstrated by the fact that shell goods from Torres Strait went as far as the New Guinea Highlands, while bird-of-paradise plumes came all the way back to the Strait. From the Aborigines at Cape York the Islanders obtained spears and spear-throwers (which the western people used for hunting instead of the bow and arrow) and red ochre. In exchange for these they gave drums and smoking pipes and perhaps occasionally cast-off canoes.

Short-distance trading between islands was even less formal. Barbara Thompson reported on the contents of a trading canoe which was sailing to the Prince of Wales group from the central islands (Moore, 1979, page 222). Unfortunately this particular canoe sank in a squall, but its cargo may be taken as typical of the trade goods involved in the local system. It comprised a large bunch of tobacco, coconuts, bananas, bamboo smoking pipes, bamboos, mats, bamboo knives, fine lines made of coconut fibre (used for catching turtle with the sucker fish), *dibi-dibis* (conus shell pendants) and coconut and bamboo water carriers. This sort of consignment might be a payment of bride-price, or for a locally made canoe, or a return for goods given earlier to help in payment of some debt.

The items were handed over in a fairly formal way. Mats were laid out and the recipient and his wife were asked to sit upon them. Then the articles were presented one by one and finally accepted before witnesses. Such local trading was carried out frequently by leading men who were canoe-owners, and often such cargoes of goods were offered in the hope of obtaining favours in the future, not just in return for some gift or service given in the past.

In Torres Strait every good deed had to be repaid, sooner or later, just as every evil action would eventually be revenged, either by magic or by raiding.

45. A *kadig* or armguard of plaited bamboo worn from wrist to elbow by bowmen to protect them from the rebound of the bowstring. Collected on Mer (Murray Island) in 1898. (Cambridge University Museum of Archaeology and Anthropology. Photograph by Henry Brewer.)

7
Warfare

Trade and warfare were opposite sides of the same coin. The friendships of the trading system were counterbalanced by enmities, some of which seem to have been traditional, though temporary hostilities could always be provoked by some foolish or accidental occurrence.

The western and central islanders appear to have been the main aggressors, whereas the northerners and the eastern people, with their gardens and settled village life were more often the victims. Nevertheless, feuding between adjacent groups was frequent and usually involved a series of reprisal raids in which heads and captives were taken. It was said that in the old days a youth did not become a man and worthy to marry until he had taken at least one head in battle.

Such feuding expeditions usually aimed at surprise, so canoes and weapons were prepared secretly by day and generally the party set out after sundown, in order to surprise the enemy at first light, while still sleeping. Pitched fights were unusual and it is probable that the death rate was not normally very high. After the raid, the victorious party would sail home to a triumphant welcome and an exultant dance ceremony, in which the heads taken would be flung around. Later there was a feast in which small pieces of cooked flesh from the cheeks were eaten as a ritual act to gain the spiritual strength of the slain.

The fighting weapons and gear of the warriors were fairly standard throughout the Strait. The weapons used were the bow and arrow, the former of bamboo and up to 2 metres (6 feet 6 inches) long with a bowstring of bamboo strip, teased out and knotted at each end. Arrows had a barbed hardwood head 30-40 cm (12-16 inches) long, usually carved and infilled with white ochre in the stylised forms of human heads, crocodiles, snakes and other motifs. The shaft, into which the head was bound, was of reed or fine bamboo about 40-50 cm (16-20 inches) long. On their bow arm warriors wore an armguard of woven bamboo strip or plant fibre which extended from wrist to elbow and protected them from the rebound of the bow string (figure 45).

The other weapon in general use was the stone-headed club (figure 46). The head was usually disc-shaped and of fine-grained volcanic stone, but some examples have four knobs and are made of coarse granitic rock. Probably all of these club heads were

46. (Above and below) Stone-headed club (*gaba-gaba*) with sling from the central islands. The disc-shaped head is ground from smooth grey volcanic stone. The handle is bamboo. The head is held on with binding and the grip end is illustrated to show incised decoration. Collected on Yam (Turtle Backed Island) in 1888. (Compare drawing of a warrior in figure 48.) (Cambridge University Museum of Archaeology and Anthropology. Photograph by Henry Brewer.)

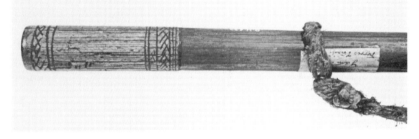

imported from mainland New Guinea, but the finishing may have been done on Yam Island, where there are still rocks with extensive grinding grooves on them. The handles were of bamboo or hardwood and were often decorated with incised designs.

A bamboo knife was used for cutting off heads and a loop of bamboo strip for carrying them. These were worn slung from the shoulder.

The accroutrements of warriors included cassowary-feather head-dresses (figure 47 and see figures 44 and 48), the *mai* or *dibi-dibi* shell chest ornaments and a triangular melo-shell phallocrypt suspended from a hairstring belt. Armbands, leg-

47. (Above) Casso-
wary-feather head-
dress (*sam*) worn by
warriors for war-
fare. Collected in
the eastern islands
in 1898. (Compare
head-dresses in fig-
ures 44 and 48)
(Cambridge Univer-
sity Museum of Ar-
chaeology and An-
thropology. Photo-
graph by Henry
Brewer.)

48. (Right) A. C.
Haddon drew this
warrior in full fight-
ing gear at Tutu
(Warrior Island) in
1888. (Haddon Arc-
hive, Cambridge
University Library.)

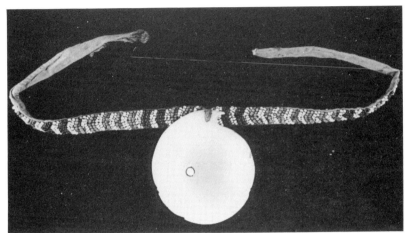

49. This unusual *dibi-dibi* conus-shell breast ornament has a gleaming 'eye' of pearlshell inlaid in the centre. The suspension band is decorated with red, white and blue trade beads. Collected on Nagir (Mount Ernest Island) in 1888. (Museum of Mankind. Photograph by Henry Brewer.)

bands and other festive adornments (as described in chapter 5) were worn as desired. In the central islands only were boar tusks gripped between the teeth, to give a fierce appearance, as is shown in the sketch of a warrior (figure 48).

Repellent and cruel as some of these practices may appear today, there can be no doubt that they inured the young men to fear and induced group solidarity, an important matter when people were so frequently scattered far and wide in the search for food and in trading pursuits. The women and children were, of course, the main sufferers, as is always the case in a raiding situation, but it seems that captives were usually married or adopted by members of the victorious group.

The net effect of both warfare and trading was to spread genes and ideas, songs and dances through the scattered communities of the Strait, to the benefit of all.

8
Post-contact developments

Even before they had their first substantial contact with Europeans in the 1840s, the Islanders had obtained some European goods, particularly iron, in the form of hatchets, barbed fishhooks, wire, nails and chains, from passing ships and wrecks. For this reason it is difficult to determine whether articles recorded as 'traditional' were manufactured with traditional tools of wood, shell, bone and stone. All the early accounts of contact stress that what the Islanders always wanted to barter for was iron, which they called *maleel* or *malili*. The other European items they sought eagerly were empty bottles and tins, biscuits and tobacco. At first they did not realise that these were all goods manufactured many hundreds or thousands of miles away, but thought that the 'white ghosts' had more powerful magic than they had. This is implicit in the 'ghost ship dance' song quoted in chapter 4.

Relations with the surveying expeditions of 1845-50 were friendly and extensive; some crew members even took the trouble to acquire the rudiments of the Torres Strait languages. However, subsequent contacts in the period 1850-70, which is poorly documented, were much less pleasant. At this time many entrepreneurs came to the Strait for considerable periods seeking pearlshell, trochus and trepang. The Islanders were not only coerced and harried to work for these people, they were also introduced to European liquor and diseases. Undoubtedly there were also many lethal clashes.

When the London Missionary Society began to establish its stations on the main islands from 1871 onwards, the missionaries found the people very willing to settle down under any sort of protection and equally ready to adopt the 'magic' of the whites. Nevertheless they did resist the destruction of their traditional sacred objects and managed to keep them hidden. By the time Professor Haddon visited the Strait (in 1888 and 1898) they had virtually all become enthusiastic Christians and were even ready to hand over to him objects that were still highly regarded for the sake of preservation.

Many of the artefacts in the Haddon collections incorporate European materials, such as the trade beads in figure 49 and the beads and cotton cloth strips in figure 41. Ceremonial objects and dance ornaments were even made of tin or cardboard, instead of turtleshell. The missionaries encouraged the continuation of some of the old handicrafts, such as basket- and mat-making, and introduced new ones, for example patchwork quilting, in which some of the traditional designs were incorporated. However, on the whole the people became progressively more and more dependent on European manufactured goods and foods.

After the establishment of government administrative headquarters on Thursday Island in 1877 a thriving pearling industry rapidly grew up and many Japanese, Malays and Pacific Islanders were employed as divers. In order to provide the Islanders with employment and a cash economy, the Queensland Government encouraged the island communities to purchase pearling luggers and operate them communally. This was carried out successfully until the First World War when there was a slump in the world demand for pearlshell and trochus shell and the industry never really recovered. The development of plastics and cultured pearls before and after the Second World War brought it virtually to an end.

During the Second World War many Islanders served in the Torres Strait Light Infantry, a local defence force, and there were large numbers of Australian and United States troops in the area. This broke down many of the traditional beliefs and prejudices among both Islanders and whites. After the war the Torres Strait communities were progressively granted more autonomy and state and Commonwealth funding greatly improved living conditions. By the late 1980s most island communities had good housing, electric power, television or video recorders, radio-telephone links and power boats for fishing and communication with other islands. All the main islands are visited regularly by air services from Thursday Island.

Although the bulk of the people's food is obtained from the community stores, supplied from the mainland, turtle and dugong are still caught with the harpoon and the old fish spears are still manufactured for off-shore fishing. A number of traditional foods continue to be grown, particularly bananas, coconuts and *wongai* and *nonda*, native fruits. However, lack of employment has led to a massive migration to mainland Australia and in the late 1980s the Islander population in Torres Strait itself is about 5000, whereas the number of Islanders on the mainland, chiefly in Queensland, is probably at least 15,000.

Recent research

In the 1960s and 1970s a few research workers attempted to

salvage remnant knowledge among the older Islanders. J. R. Beckett concentrated on the social and political developments in the Strait, Margaret Lawrie on myths and legends, D. Harris on subsistence strategies, and the author and R. Vanderwal on material culture and prehistory. A number of linguists worked on the languages, including Torres Strait Creole, a post-contact *lingua franca* allied to New Guinea pidgin. These efforts led to a revival of interest in the old way of life and a number of attempts were made to reconstruct the ancient dances and ceremonies (figure 50).

In the 1980s a new wave of young anthropologists, particularly from James Cook University, Townsville, directed their attention to the Strait. Interest was further stimulated because the first volume of a projected *Handbook of Aboriginal and Torres Strait Islander Material Culture* was to deal with Torres Strait and North Queensland. Therefore, detailed studies of particular aspects of Torres Strait culture were made, drawing partly on close contact with older Islanders and partly on library and archival resources.

The publication of a fully illustrated catalogue of the Haddon collections (Moore, 1984) resulted in renewed interest among the Islanders in their own traditional life and a number of island people, both old and young, began to manufacture old-time artefacts once again. These included ceremonial carvings, woven pandanus and palm-leaf items, and traditional weapons; some of these were for sale in tourist shops, others for display in community halls. There was, in addition, much talk of once again building the large dugout outrigger sailing canoes.

Also in the 1980s the Islanders began to press for the establishment of a Torres Strait Museum and Cultural Centre on Thursday Island, in which their traditional artefacts could be displayed for the interest and instruction of their own people and of Europeans. The museum had not got beyond the planning stage by 1988, due to lack of funding, but requests have been made that museums in Australia and Britain should consider the repatriation of at least some Torres Strait artefacts for eventual display.

So, after a long period of isolation and apathy, the Islanders are now regaining pride in their own heritage and appreciation of the skills of their forefathers.

The artistic tradition

Little attention has been given to either the aesthetics or the manufacturing techniques of Torres Strait arts and crafts.

50. (Above and below) A modern reconstruction of the climax of the Malu-Bomai initiation ritual on Mer (Murray Island). It was photographed by Dr J. R. Beckett in 1967. The participants took great pains to ensure that the detail of costumes, masks and so on was authentic, because they were to be filmed for a Commonwealth Government documentary called *The Islanders.*

Haddon's attitude to this aspect of Torres Strait life would nowadays be categorised as that of a material culture specialist. He was concerned to analyse decorative motifs and to try to trace their origins, and he was interested in the way artefacts were used. However, he was not able to study manufacturing methods in any detail, nor did he make any attempt to evaluate the Islanders' appreciation of the aesthetic qualities of their art.

The only writer to consider Torres Strait art *per se* was Douglas Fraser, who published *Torres Strait Sculpture; a Study in Oceanic Primitive Art* in 1978, though it was closely based on his PhD thesis completed in 1961. It deals mainly with the turtleshell and wooden masks in museum collections all over the world and is marred by Fraser's extreme diffusionist bias. In *Torres Strait Sculpture* and in his general work, *Primitive Art*, published in 1962, he classified Torres Strait art as having been derived from 'the aquatic tradition' of Chinese art of some three thousand years ago, which he considered to have been characterised by 'masks representing voracious animals, with long snouts' (page 120).

While it is undeniable that Pacific art in general must owe some debt to ancient China, it seems scarcely supportable to link Torres Strait art directly with a tradition in an area many thousands of kilometres distant and three thousand years in the past. One would require a series of definite connecting links, in both time and space, in order to accept this hypothesis as valid. Fraser, surprisingly, almost entirely ignored the wood and stone carvings of Torres Strait, which might more properly be classed as sculptures and in many ways are more aesthetically satisfying than the masks.

There are, however, definite affinities between the art of Torres Strait and that of the south coast of New Guinea, particularly the Gulf of Papua and the Marind-Anim culture of southern Irian Jaya. Nevertheless, neither of these areas can boast the production of composite turtleshell artefacts, nor of the delicate pearlshell creations so highly prized by both the Islanders and the Papuans. The art of Torres Strait is a unique entity evolved within the remarkably closed and self-contained world of the Torres Strait islands. How far the religious beliefs and their associated artefacts stretch back in time is not yet known, but there is a good chance that archaeological work already commenced in the Strait will eventually elucidate some, at least, of the problems associated with the Islanders and their art.

When handling and photographing the whole range of Torres

Strait aretfacts in the Haddon collections, the author was continually impressed by the aesthetic effectiveness of simplified shapes, often allied with delicate and complex decorations, particularly in ceremonial and magical objects. Especially satisfying are the silhouetted human figure used in tobacco gardens (figure 19), the double sea-eagle canoe figurehead (figure 20) and the stone rain-magic figures (figure 23), all of which are greatly enhanced by the soft ochre colours with which they are painted. The turtleshell mask on the cover of this book, which is in the Australian Museum, is surely a masterpiece of intricate details, each of which contributes to a most satisfying whole with a real personality of its own. In contrast, the Australian Museum's *warup* drum (figure 30) allies a pure perfection of form to excellence of acoustical function.

Even in their utilitarian everyday artefacts, the Islanders achieved an almost Scandinavian feeling in their essential rightness for their particular purpose. Just to cite two examples, the turtleshell fishhook and the harpoon head in figure 11 are quintessentially functional, yet have a simple beauty obviously developed over many generations of makers and passed down from father to son.

Finally, the Torres Strait canoe must be considered not only as an extremely efficient machine vital to the Torres Strait way of life, but also as a thing of beauty and a product of the highest standards of both art and craft. To support this status, a remark made by O. W. Brierly, artist on the *Rattlesnake*, when he first sighted a fully rigged Torres Strait canoe under sail in 1848, may be quoted: 'I had long admired but I had never till now seen anything that realised so much the idea of beauty' (Moore, 1979, page 48).

It is to be hoped that the present marked revival of interest in the traditional arts and crafts of the region will result in the Islanders once again applying their outstanding artistic abilities to producing beautiful things, both for their own fulfilment and for the aesthetic pleasure of all peoples.

9
Museums

The following are the main collections of Torres Strait artefacts held by museums in the British Isles and Australia. Intending visitors are advised to check in advance regarding the availability of material, since Torres Strait collections are not often put on public display.

British Isles

Cambridge University Museum of Archaeology and Anthropology, Downing Street, Cambridge CB2 3DZ. Telephone: 0223 337733 or 333516. Collections made by the Cambridge Expedition of 1898.

Glasgow Art Gallery and Museum, Kelvingrove, Glasgow G3 8AG. Telephone: 041-357 3929. Collection made by Robert Bruce while in Torres Strait in the late nineteenth century.

Horniman Museum, London Road, Forest Hill, London SE23 3PQ. Telephone: 01-699 1872, 2339 or 4911. Subsidiary collection from A. C. Haddon's first visit.

Museum of Mankind (the Ethnography Department of the British Museum), 6 Burlington Gardens, London W1X 2EX. Telephone: 01-323 8043. The basic collection made by A. C. Haddon in Torres Strait in 1888-9.

National Museum of Ireland, Kildare Street, Dublin 2. Telephone: 01-765521. Subsidiary collection from A. C. Haddon's first visit.

Pitt Rivers Museum, South Parks Road, Oxford OX1 3PP. Telephone: 0865 270927. Subsidiary collection of 1898.

Australia

The Australian Museum, 6-8 College Street, Sydney, New South Wales 2000. Major Torres Strait collection.

Macleay Museum of Natural History, University of Sydney, Sydney, New South Wales 2006.

National Museum of Victoria, 258-321 Russell Street, Melbourne, Victoria 3000.

Queensland Museum, Cultural Centre, Southbank, Brisbane, Queensland 4000. Major Torres Strait collection.

Tasmanian Museum and Art Gallery, 5 Argyle Street, Hobart, Tasmania 7000.

10
Further reading

Allen, J., and Corris, P. (editors). *The Journal of John Sweatman: a Nineteenth Century Surveying Voyage in North Australia and Torres Strait*. Queensland University Press, 1977.

Beckett, J. *The Torres Strait Islanders: Custom and Colonialism*. Cambridge University Press, 1987.

Fraser, D. *Primitive Art*. Thames and Hudson, London, 1962.

Fraser, D. *Torres Strait Sculpture: A Study in Oceanic Primitive Art*. Garland, New York and London, 1978.

Haddon, A. C. *Headhunters, Black, White and Brown*. Methuen, London, 1901.

Moore, D. R. *Islanders and Aborigines at Cape York: an Ethnographic Reconstruction Based on the 1848-1850 'Rattlesnake' Journals of O. W. Brierly and Information He Obtained from Barbara Thompson*. Australian Institute of Aboriginal Studies, Canberra; Humanities Press, New Jersey, 1979.

Moore, D. R. *The Torres Strait Collections of A. C. Haddon: a Descriptive Catalogue*. British Museum Publications, London, 1984.

Reynolds, B. (editor). *Australian Material Culture: a Handbook of Aboriginal and Torres Strait Islander Material Culture*, volume 1 'North-east'. Australian Institute of Aboriginal Studies, Canberra, in preparation.

Walker, D. (editor). *Bridge and Barrier: the Natural and Cultural History of Torres Strait*. Department of Geography, Australian National University, Canberra, 1972.

Index

Page numbers in italics refer to illustrations

Adzes 17
Axes 17
Armguards *49*, 50
Armet 43-5, *46*, 51
Australian Aborigines 8, *9*, 11, 23, 48
Bags and baskets 12, 14, *14*, *15*, *39*, 40, 55
Ball games 40
Bamboo 17, 20, *21*, *38*, 39-40, *39*, 49, *49*, 50
Bananas 22, 30, 49, 55
Beads, trade *46*, *53*, 54
Belts 41, *42*
Bird-of-paradise 48
Blackwood, Captain F. P. 5
Bligh, William 5
Boar tusk 17, 48, *52*, 53
Bomai 23, *57*
Bow and arrow 11, 48, 50
Bullroarer 30
Bramble, HM Schooner 5, 8
Breast ornaments *41*, *44*, *45*, *47*
Brierly, O. W. 8, *19*, 20
Cables 18
Cannibalism 50
Canoes *9*, *10*, 11, *13*, 18-19, *19*, 20, 29, *29*, *30*, 48-9, 56, *56*, 59
Cassowary feathers *cover*, 25, *25*, 37, 41, *47*, 48, 51, *52*
Catscradle 40
Cicatrisation *32*, 45
Clam shell 17, 41, *47*
Clubs 48, 50, 51, *51*
Coconuts *17*, 22, 49, 55
Combs 41, *43*
Conch shell 40
Conus shell 41, 45, *47*, 49, 51
Cook, James 5
Cooking 17, 21, 49, *52*, *53*
Cookpots, shell 17, 21
Cord 18, *18*, 19, 49
Dancing 37-8
Darnley Island *10*
Digging sticks *16*, 17, 22
Drills 43
Drums 11, 23, 25-6, *36*, 37, 48, 59
Dugong *18*, 19, 20, 21, *21*, *30*, 55
Ear-piercing 41
Ear weight 41, *43*

Earth oven 21
Edwards, E. 5
Evans Bay *9*
Figureheads, canoe 29, *29, 30,* 59
Fire 22
Fishhooks *18,* 20-1, 59
Fishing 14, 16, 18, 20
Fish traps 20, *21*
Flinders, Matthew 5
Flutes 17
Fly, HMS 5
Fly River 11, 48
Four Brothers, the 23
Fraser, Douglas 58
Games 40
Gardens 11, *16,* 17, 22, 29, *34*
Ghosts 5, 26, 29
Haddon, Alfred Cort 9, 10, *13, 14, 24,* 25, *34,* 45, *47, 52,* 54, 56, 58, 59
Hair styles 41
Harpoons 17, 18, *18,* 20, *55,* 59
Head-dresses 12, 41, *42,* 51
Headhunting 11, 12, 19, 48, 50-1, *52*
Hero cults 11, 12, 23
Hoes *16,* 17, 22
Initiation 12, 25-6, *57*
Jervis Island *13, 15, 21,* 23
Jukes, J. B. 8
Kala Lagaw Ya (language) 11
Kulka 23
Kwoiam 23
Lewis, C. M. 5
London Missionary Society 8, 54
Mabuiag (language) 11
MacGillivray, J. 8
Magic 12, *28,* 29-35, *29, 30, 31, 32, 34*
Malu 23, 57
Mangrove, red 14, 21
Marind-Anim 58
Markai (ghosts) 5, 26, 29
Masks *cover,* 12, 23-7, *24, 25, 27, 28, 36,* 37-8, *57,* 58, 59
Mats 12, 15-17, *15,* 26, 49, 55
Medicine men 29-35
Melville, H. S. 8, *10*
Meriam (people) 11, 23
Meriam Mir (language) 11
Mortuary ceremonies 12, 26-9
Mummification 29

Nautilus shell 41, *44*, *45*
Necklaces 41, *44*, 45, *46*
Ochres 45, 48, 50
Oysters 15
Papua, Gulf of 58
Pearlshell 8, *21*, 41, *44*, *45*, 54-5, 58
Pendants 41, 43, *44*, *47*, *51*
Phallocrypt *47*, 51
Population 5, 55
Queensland Government 8, 55
Rattles *cover*, 24, *24*, *27*
Rattlesnake, HMS 5, 8
Ropes 18
Sago 22
Sau 23
Scarification, body *32*, 45, 47
Shellfish *14*, 15
Shell tools 12, *16*, 17, *21*
Sigai 23
Skirts 12, *24*, *41*, *47*, 57
Smoking pipes *9*, 17, *38*, 39, 49
Spears 20, 48, 55
Stanley, Captain Owen 5, *9*
Stone carvings 12, 26, 29, *30*, *31*, *34*, 35, 58, 59
String games 40
Sucker fish 20, *33*
Sweatman, John 8
Taro 22
Thompson, Barbara 37, 49
Thursday Island 8, *24*, 55-6
Tobacco *10*, *38*, 39, 49
Tops, spinning *39*, 40
Torres, Luis Vaez de 5
Torres Strait Creole (language) 5
Torres Strait Light Infantry 55
Totems 23, *25*, *26*, *27*, *32*, 35
Trade 11, *16*, 48-9
Trepang 8, 54
Trochus shell 8, 54-5
Turtle 18, 20, 21, 25, 43, *47*, 55, 58
Waiet *34*, 35
Warfare 50-3
Water 17
Water carriers 17, *17*, 49
Weapons 11, 48, 50-3, *51*, 52
Wigs *cover*, 41
World War, Second 55
Yams 14, *14*, *15*, 21, 22